Sunshine

Pupil's Book 3

Erarbeitet von
Inga Bensmann (Weyhe)
Helga Haudeck (Ludwigsburg)
Nadine Kerler (Ulm)
Caroline Schröder (München)

Auf der Grundlage der Ausgabe von
Tanja Beattie
Birgit Hollbrügge
Stefanie Keller
Nadine Kerler
Ulrike Kraaz
Caroline Schröder

Cornelsen

Contents

listen   draw or write   listen to the CD,

talk   play   Track 1 (Schüler-CD)/

read   extra   Track 2 (Lehrer-CD)

1 Read the words. Find the pictures.
computer, cowboy, hamburger, laptop, skateboard.

 **2** Do you know more words? Make a poster.

Think. Pair. Share.

> **! Note**
>
> | 🇩🇪 | 🇬🇧 |
> |---|---|
> | Cornflakes | cornflakes |
> | Jeans | jeans |

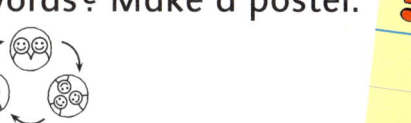

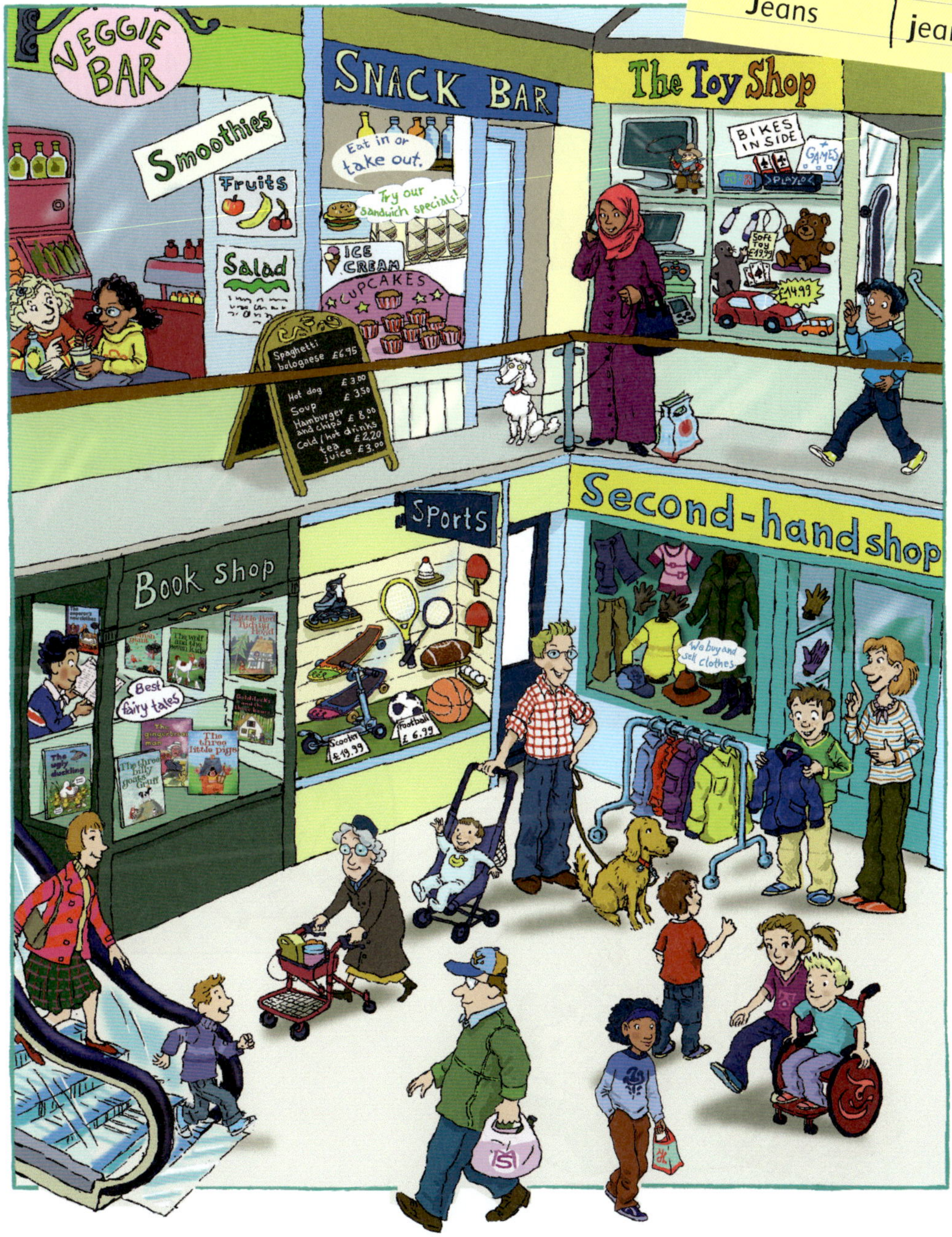

1 Listen to the rhyme. Point to the pictures.

⭐ Say the rhyme with a partner. Do the actions.

Meeting friends

 **Note**

In Großbritannien sind alle Briefkästen rot. Fallen dir weitere Besonderheiten auf?

1 Talk about the picture.

2 Listen to your teacher. Point to the numbers.

3 Listen to your teacher. Say the colours.

4 Listen. Where do Samir, Harry, Kate and Emily live?

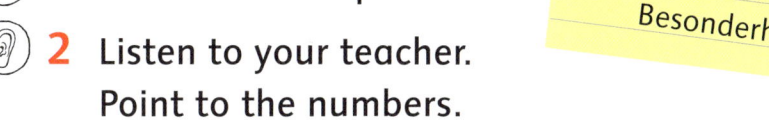

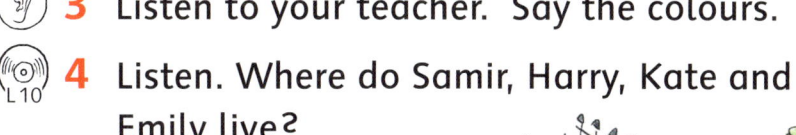

1 Listen. Point to the numbers.

2 Say the numbers.

3 Play 'hopscotch'.

4 Explain.

You start, Emily.

1, 2, …

Good, Emily.

10, 9, 8, …

Oops!

5 Read the dialogue with a partner.

What's your favourite colour?

My favourite colour is green.

 1 Talk about Harry's family.

2 Listen. Point to the pictures.
L 11

This is Harry's …

Number … is Harry's …

I'm 9 years old. How old are you?

Note

- Find more family words in a dictionary or on the Internet.
- Make a poster of your family tree. Talk about it.

Let's talk

3 Read the dialogue. Talk to a partner.

⭐ More: Make up your own dialogue.

Have you got a brother?

Yes, I have.

Have you got a sister?

No, I haven't.

1 Look at the map. Where do they speak English?

Talk about the colours and the flags.

⭐ Listen to your partner. Point to the country.

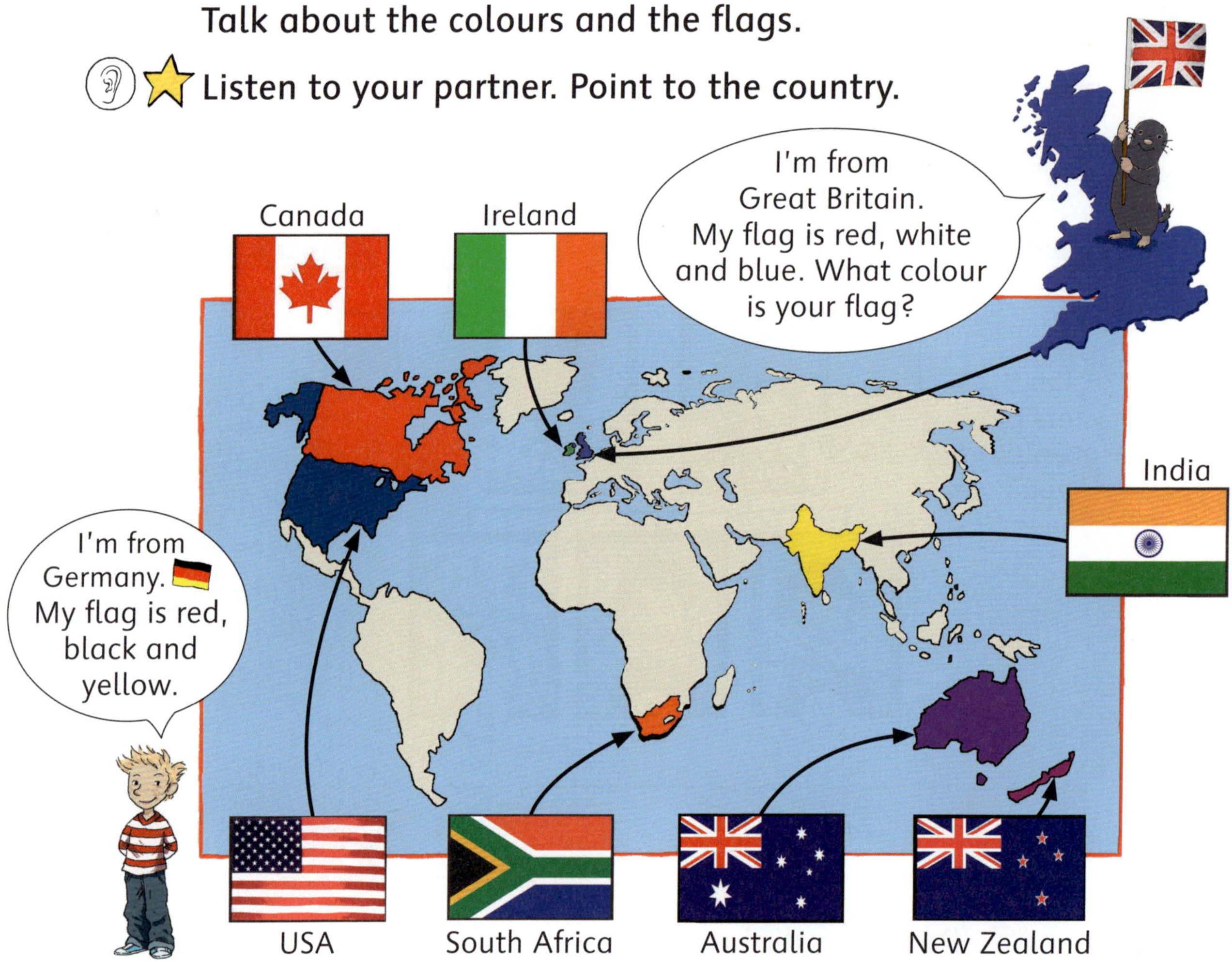

Canada

Ireland

I'm from Great Britain. My flag is red, white and blue. What colour is your flag?

India

I'm from Germany. My flag is red, black and yellow.

USA   South Africa   Australia   New Zealand

⭐ **What about you?**

I live in Great Britain. My family is from …

There's … / There are …

 1 Talk about the picture.

 2 Listen. What pets have the children got?

 ⭐ Do a class survey. Think. Pair. Share.

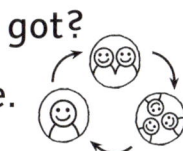

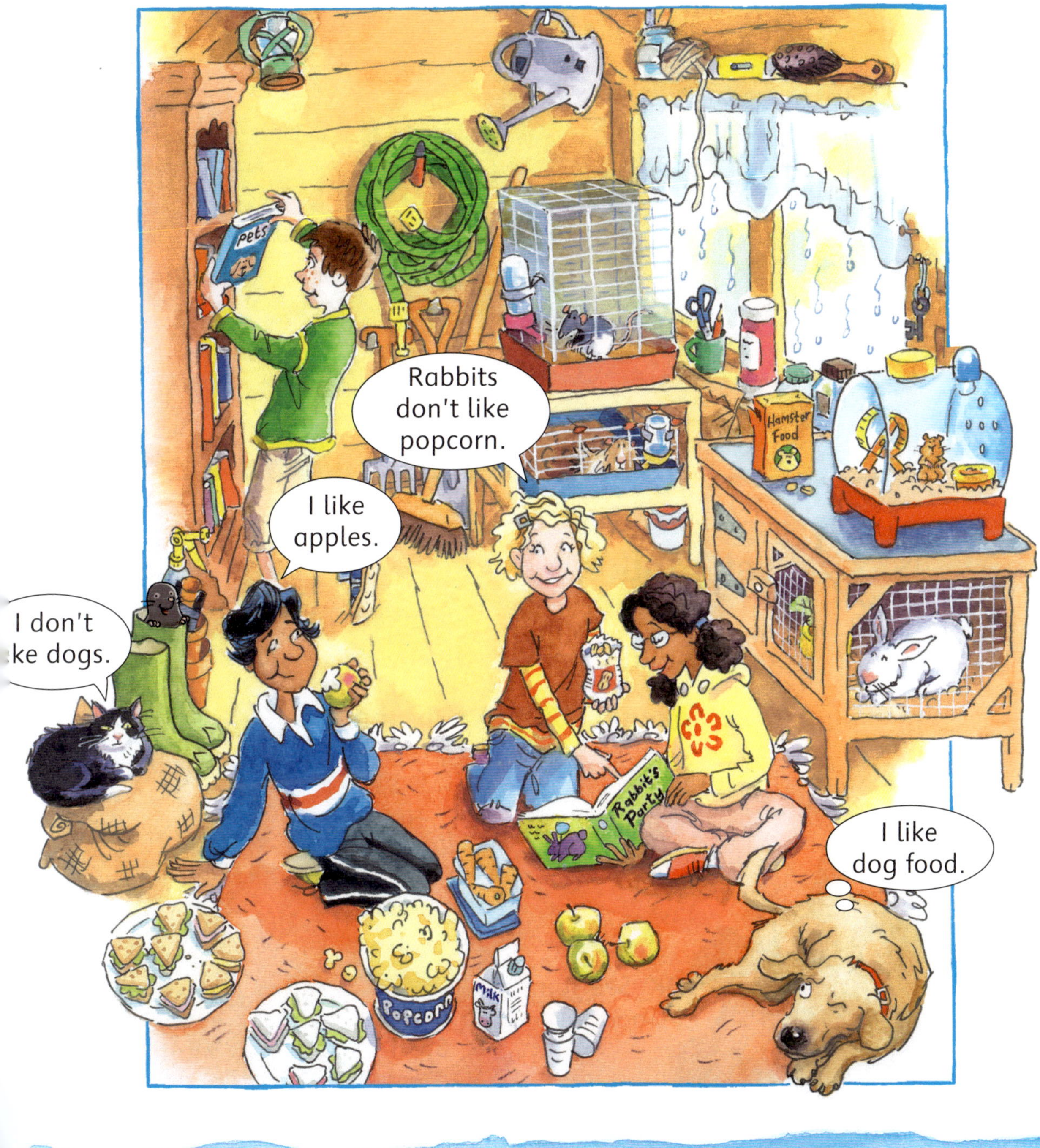

L 18

1 Listen. Who is on the telephone?

Let's talk

2 Read the dialogue. Talk to a partner.

⭐ More: Make up your own dialogue.

1 Read the story.

2 Act out the story.

⭐ Write a party invitation.

📖 **1** Read the words and sentences.

 2 Explain.

 👥 **3** Play the game.

START

Go to the matching word.

Go to the matching picture.

Take a card. Say a sentence.

Miss a turn.

dog

rabbit

apple

rat

cat

carrot

guinea pig

peanuts

hamster

lettuce

FINISH

 1 Listen. Point to the pictures.

sheep dog

rescue dog

police dog

guide dog

 2 Read the speech bubbles with a partner.

 3 Do the dog actions with your partner. Guess the actions. Take turns.

4 Explain. Play the game with your class.

I'm happy.

I'm sleepy.

I'm scared.

I'm sad.

I'm hungry.

Watch the film.

 2

Fächerübergreifendes Lernen: „Arts and crafts", s. HRU, S. 287-288

 1 Talk about the picture.

 2 Listen to the song. Point to the school things in the picture.

⭐ Where are the school things? Write sentences:
The chair is next to the table. Think. Pair. Share.

> *Where's Mr Mole?*
> *Where can he be?*
> *Where's Mr Mole?*
> *Let me see.*
>
> *Is he in the school bag?*
> *Is he on the book?*
> *Or under the table?*
> *Let's have a look.*
>
> *No! Not there!*

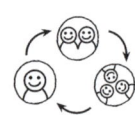 **Note**

In Großbritannien gibt es in vielen Klassen einen zweiten Lehrer oder eine zweite Lehrerin. Diese Person nennt man *classroom assistant*.

1 Read the texts.

 2 Explain.

 3 Play the game in groups of four.

 Note

Make a video.
Explain the rules.

(1) Take five cards from your word box.

(2) Put your cards on the table.

(3) Shuffle all the cards.

(4) Give five cards to each player.

(5) Ask questions.

Can I have a pencil, please?

Here you are.

Have you got a ruler, please?

Sorry, I haven't got a ruler.

The player with the most cards wins.

Story: Jack's bad day

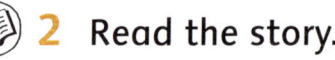

1 Listen to the story.

2 Read the story.

3 What happens in the end?

Think. Pair. Share.

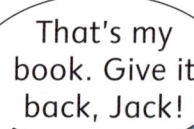

More to explore: School in Britain

 1 Talk about the pictures.

 2 Listen. Point to the pictures.
L32

 3 Read the texts.

 **Note**

In Großbritannien schaust du zuerst nach rechts, wenn du eine Straße überquerst. Weißt du warum?

A **lollipop man** helps children cross the road.

Some children walk to school with the **walking bus**.

This is a **school building**.

School starts with **assembly**.

 4 Make a school badge. You need:

cardboard	felt tips or coloured pencils	scissors	a safety pin	sticky tape

① Draw a circle on the cardboard.
   Write the name of your school. Colour the badge.

② Cut out the badge.

③ Tape a safety pin to the back of your badge.

Watch the film. **5** Explain.

What I can do and say

A word web

family

brother
mother
father
sister

grandmother, cousin, …

This is my …
I've got a …
I haven't got a …

Have you got a …?

Make your own word web.   Think. Pair. Share.

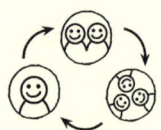

friends and family

school

pets

My name is … · I'm … years old. · I live in … · This is my … ·
It's a … · It likes … · What colour is …/do you like? · I like/
don't like … · My favourite … · My mother's/dog's/… name
is … · I'm … · What about you? · Where are you from? ·
I'm from … · I'm in class … · My teacher is … · Can I have …,
please? · Here you are. · Thanks. · You're welcome.

What can you do or say in English? Think!

I can …

… say the words.

… write the words.

… ask and answer questions.

**What do you want
to be better at?**

What I can do and say

You can find more words

- in your Pupil's Book.

- in your Activity Book.

- in a dictionary.

- on the Internet

Play 'pick a pair' with your mini picture cards.

Game for two players. You need: Two sets of mini picture cards.

1. Put the cards on the table.

A dog!

2. Pick two cards. Turn them over. Name the cards.

It's a pair!

3. Two cards the same? Keep the pair and play again.

It's my turn!

4. Not the same? Put them back again.

The player with the most cards wins.

4   The second-hand shop

1 Talk about the picture.

2 Listen to your partner. Point.

⭐ Play 'I spy'. Explain.

! Note

jeans – Jeans

Can you find more words that are the same in German and English?

There's … / There are …

Look! I'm wearing a dress!

Closed

1 Listen to your teacher. Who is it?

 2 Choose one child. Talk to a partner.

 ⭐ What is Samir wearing?
Write: *He is wearing ...*

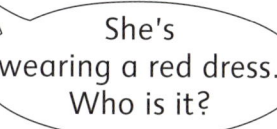

Sarah   Harry   Kate

Samir   Emily   John

Let's talk

1 Read the dialogue. Talk to a partner.

⭐ More: Make up your own dialogue.

2 Talk to your partner.

Do you like …?

⭐ Write the words. Look at your word list (page 41–44).

Story: A funny boy

Note

Dress up.
Make a video.

1 Read the story.

2 Act out the story.

 **S 13 L 40** **1** Listen to the story. Point to the pictures.

 2 Talk about the pictures. How does the story end?

①

②

③

④

⑤

⑥

 ⭐ Read the rhyme with a partner.
Find the matching pictures.
What about picture 6?

 Note

Find the rhyming words.
boat – goat
…
Make a list.

My tie is a scarf for a cold giraffe.

My shirt's on a boat as a sail for a goat.

My shoe is a house for a little white mouse.

One of my socks is a bed for a fox.

My belt helped a dog who was crossing a bog.

1 Talk about school uniforms.
What is the boy wearing?
What is the girl wearing?

The girl is wearing …

a cardigan · a pullover ·
a shirt · shoes · a skirt ·
socks · a tie · trousers

Note

In Großbritannien tragen die Kinder Uniformen in der Schule.
In welchen Ländern gibt es noch Schuluniformen? Schaue im Internet.

 2 Listen. Point to the pictures.

 ⭐ Listen to your partner. Which school is it?

①

②

③

Watch the film.

Queen's School

Blake School

Swanage School

S 14
L 43

1 Listen to the song. Point to the pictures.

2 Sing the song. Do the actions.

Football, music, books, TV,
bikes and comics, friends, PC.
Tell me, tell me,
What about you?
Do you like the things I do?

Playing football
is what I like.
Watching TV,
riding my bike.

Listening to music,
tapping my feet,
meeting friends
in the street.

Reading books
and comics, too.
Playing computer
games.
What about you?

I like
meeting friends.
What do you
like?

Let's talk

1 Read the dialogue. Talk to a partner.

⭐ More: Make up your own dialogue.

That's boring.

What about listening to music?

Great idea!

 2 Listen to the rhyme. Point to the pictures.

 3 Read the rhyme.

⭐ Present the rhyme. Think. Pair. Share.

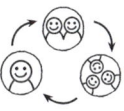

Where's the cat? Where's the cat?
Is it in the living room – watching TV?
Is it in the kitchen – drinking my tea?

Where's the cat? Where's the cat?
Is it in the bedroom – eating my shoe?
Is it in the bathroom – playing with shampoo?

Where's the cat? Where's the cat?
There it is – sleeping in Mum's favourite hat.

1 **1** Where is Harry? Where is Kate?

2 **2** Talk to your partner.

⭐ Write sentences: *There is / There are …*

In house number 1, Harry/… is in the kitchen/…

Story: The babysitters

1 Listen to the story.
Point to the pictures.

2 Read the story.

Here's a great CD.

I don't like listening to music.

2

Oh, this is boring.

1

What about playing football?

Great idea! Where's my football?

3

Is your football in your bedroom?

No, it isn't in my bedroom.

4

Not in the living room, Nick!

Oh dear. Sorry!

5

3 Listen to the story. What do they not say?

1

What about meeting friends?

2

What about playing computer games?

3

What about watching TV?

1 Look at the pictures.
Read the names of the games.

2 Talk about the games.

3 Listen. Point to the pictures.

Playground games:

connect 4 · skipping ·
hide-and-seek · tag

4 Read the rules. Explain.

5 Play 'rock, paper, scissors'.

Note

Was spielst du gerne auf dem Schulhof? Vergleiche.

① Say and do.

Rock, paper, scissors. Show!

② Who is the winner?

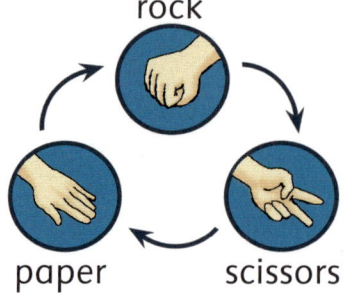

rock

paper   scissors

③ Two hands the same?

Play again!

Fächerübergreifendes Lernen: „P.E. (Sports)", s. HRU, S. 293-294

1 Talk about the picture.

 2 Listen to your teacher. Find the numbers.

⭐ Talk to a partner. How many dogs / tables / scooters / ... can you see?

There's ... / There are ...

I can see ...

6

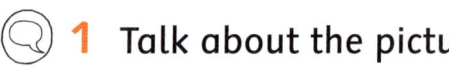
How much is / are the …?

1 Talk about the picture. It's / They're …

2 Listen. What does the boy say?

⭐ Write a shopping list.

MY SHOPPING LIST
- 1 apple

Let's talk

3 Read the dialogue. Talk to a partner.

⭐ More: Make up your own dialogue.

S 19
L 57

1 Listen to the story.

2 Read the speech bubbles.

3 Say what is right and what is wrong.

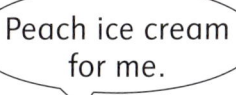

 1 Look at the signs. Read the sentences. Match.

 2 Talk about the signs.

 ⭐ Draw a new park sign. Write a sentence.

Think. Pair. Share.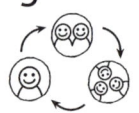

Note

Find more signs.
Take photos.
 Explain.

1

2

3

4

5

6

Wheelchair access	No ball games
Please keep off the grass.	No bikes
No horse riding.	
No dogs	

Can you dig holes in the park?

Watch the film.

Special days: Birthday

1 Talk about the picture.

2 Write a birthday card.

3 Sing the song. Do the actions.

S 20
L 59
4 Listen to the song. Point to the pictures.

Someone's birthday is today, is today, is today.
Someone's birthday is today, and it's our …

Let's prepare a birthday cake,
birthday cake, birthday cake.
Let's prepare a birthday cake,
just for our …

Add a candle for each year,
for each year, for each year.
Add a candle for each year,
just for our …

Make a special birthday card,
birthday card, birthday card.
Make a special birthday card,
just for our …

 **Note**

Zum Geburtstag tragen
englische Kinder gerne selbst
gebastelte Hüte oder Kronen.
Wie feierst du deinen
Geburtstag?

Happy
birthday!

Special days: Christmas

🇬🇧 **Note**

Kinder in Großbritannien hängen am 24.12. Strümpfe auf. Diese werden über Nacht gefüllt.
Kennst Du weitere Besonderheiten?

💬 **1** Look at the picture. Talk about the Christmas things.

💬 **2** Look at the pictures. Find the Christmas things in the house.

I wish you a merry Christmas and a happy New Year!

1 Talk about the pictures. What is beautiful? What is bad?

> sun · bees · Earth · animals · mountains · birds · river · trees ·
> flowers · sea · cars · bad air · fire · plastic (bottles/bags)

2 Read and talk about the posters.

3 Make your own poster.

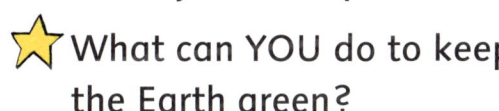
What can YOU do to keep the Earth green?

 Note

- Find out more about Earth Day. When is it?
- Can you find songs or books about Earth Day? Search for: "Earth Day song" or "Earth Day books for children".
- There is a love song to the Earth. Can you find it on the Internet?

1 Make your own Easter bunny.

You need:

 1 piece of square paper	 scissors

Fold and cut the paper.

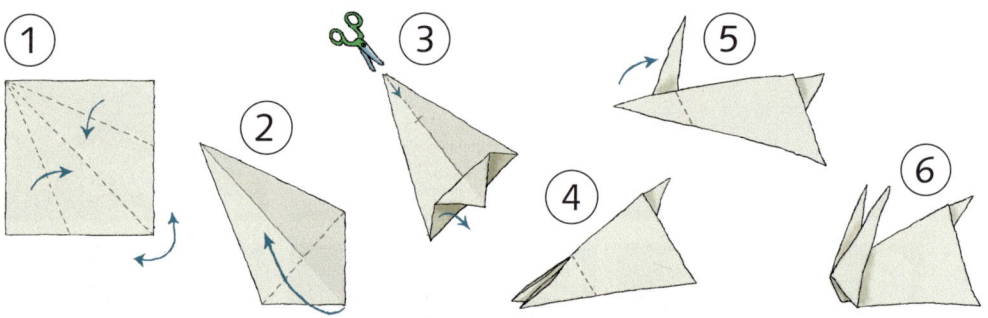

① ② ③ ④ ⑤ ⑥

 2 Listen to the Easter rhyme.

 3 Say the rhyme.

 **Note**

In England essen die Leute zu Ostern *hot cross buns*. Was isst du gerne zu Ostern?

Here's a bunny
with ears so funny,
and here is his hole in the ground.
And when a noise he hears,
he pricks up his ears,
and hops in his hole in the ground.

I like Easter eggs. What do you like for Easter?

I like hot cross buns.

What I can do and say

A word web

clothes

dress
jeans
pullover
shirt
shoes

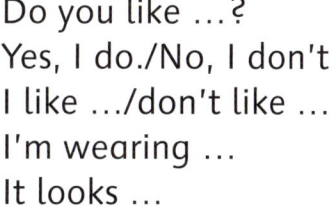

Do you like …?
Yes, I do./No, I don't.
I like …/don't like …
I'm wearing …
It looks …

cold …   How many … have you got?

Make your own word web.   Think. Pair. Share.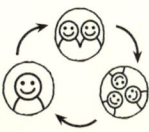

hobbies

special days

fruit and drinks

Can I help you? · Yes, please. · No, thank you. · I'd like… ·
Can I have … please? · Here you are. · You're welcome. ·
How much is/are …? · How many …? · What's your hobby? ·
Please come to my party. · Can you come to my party? · Yes,
I can. · No, thank you. · I'm sorry. · That's ok. · What about
you? · I wish you a merry Christmas and a happy New Year! ·
Happy birthday!

What can you do or say in English? Think!

 … say the words.

I can …   ✏ … write the words.   **What do you want
to be better at?**

 … ask and answer questions.

What I can do and say

Can you write the word?

books

1 Read the word.

2 Look up.

3 Look at the word again.

4 Write down the word.

5 Check the word.

Play 'bingo' with your mini picture cards.

Game for three or more (one caller).
You need: Two sets of mini picture cards for each player.

How to play:

Mouse!

Bingo!

1 Put down six or nine cards.

2 Listen to the caller. Have you got the card? Turn it over. Listen again.

3 Have you got all cards? You are the winner.

A

apple Apfel

B

banana Banane
bedroom Schlafzimmer
behind hinter
big groß
bike Fahrrad
birthday Geburtstag
birthday cake Geburtstagskuchen
birthday card Geburtstagskarte
birthday present Geburtstagsgeschenk
black schwarz
blue blau
book Buch
boring langweilig
boy Junge
bread Brot
brother Bruder
brown braun
Bye! Tschüss!

C

can/can't können/nicht können
candle Kerze
carrot Möhre
cat Katze
chair Stuhl
cherry Kirsche
chocolate Schokolade
Christmas Weihnachten
Christmas Day Weihnachtstag (25.12.)
Christmas Eve Heiligabend (24.12.)
Christmas tree Weihnachtsbaum
class Klasse
classroom Klassenzimmer
cold kalt
colour Farbe, ausmalen
come kommen

D

dog Hund
draw zeichnen
dress Kleid, ankleiden
dress up sich verkleiden
drink Getränk, trinken

E

Easter Ostern
Easter basket Osterkorb
Easter bunny Osterhase
Easter egg Osterei

eat essen
eight acht
eighty achtzig

F

family Familie
father Vater
Father Christmas Weihnachtsmann
favourite Lieblings-
felt tip Filzstift
fifty fünfzig
fish Fisch
five fünf
food Essen
football Fußball
forty vierzig
four vier
friend Freund, Freundin
fruit Obst

G

garden shed Gartenhaus
Germany Deutschland
girl Mädchen
gloves Handschuhe
glue stick Klebstift
go gehen, fahren, laufen
good gut
grandfather Großvater
grandmother Großmutter
great toll
green grün
grey grau
guinea pig Meerschweinchen

H

hamster Hamster
happy glücklich
Happy Birthday! Herzlichen
  Glückwunsch zum Geburtstag!
hat Mütze
Hello! Hallo!
hobby Hobby
house Haus
hundred hundert
hungry hungrig

I

ice cream Eiscreme
in in
in front of vor
inline skates Inlineskates

Word list

J

jacket Jacke
jeans Jeans
juice Saft

L

lemon Zitrone
lettuce Salat
like mögen
listening to music Musik hören
living room Wohnzimmer
look (for) suchen (nach)
lunch Mittagessen
lunch box Brotdose

M

meeting friends Freunde treffen
Merry Christmas! Frohe
  Weihnachten!
milk Milch
mother Mutter
mouse Maus

N

name Name
next to neben
nine neun
ninety neunzig
number Zahl

O

on auf
one eins
orange orange, Apfelsine

P

peach Pfirsich
peanuts Erdnüsse
pen Füller
pencil Bleistift
pencil case Federmappe
pencil sharpener Bleistiftspitzer
pet Haustier
pink rosa
play spielen
playing computer games
    Computerspiele spielen
playing football Fußball spielen
plum Pflaume
pound (£) Pfund (britisches Geld)
pullover Pullover

R

rabbit Kaninchen

(continued)

rat Ratte
read lesen
red rot
room Zimmer
rubber Radiergummi
ruler Lineal

S

scarf Schal
school Schule
school bag Schultasche
scissors Schere
scooter Roller
seven sieben
seventy siebzig
shirt Hemd
shoes Schuhe
shop Laden
sister Schwester
six sechs
sixty sechzig
skateboard Skateboard
skirt Rock
small klein
socks Socken
Sorry! Entschuldigung!
strawberry Erdbeere

T

T-shirt T-Shirt
teacher Lehrer, Lehrerin
ten zehn
thirsty durstig
thirty dreißig
three drei
tomato Tomate
trousers Hose
twenty zwanzig
two zwei

U

under unter

V

very sehr

W

watching TV fernsehen
wear tragen, anhaben
white weiß

Y

yellow gelb

Word list

A

acht eight
achtzig eighty
anhaben wear
ankleiden dress
Apfel apple
Apfelsine orange
auf on
ausmalen colour

B

Banane banana
blau blue
Bleistift pencil
Bleistiftspitzer pencil sharpener
braun brown
Brot bread
Brotdose lunch box
Bruder brother
Buch book

C

Computerspiele spielen playing
  computer games

D

Deutschland Germany
drei three
dreißig thirty
durstig thirsty

E

eins one
Eiscreme ice cream
Entschuldigung! Sorry!
Erdbeere strawberry
Erdnüsse peanuts
essen eat
Essen food

F

fahren go
Fahrrad bike
Familie family
Farbe colour
Federmappe pencil case
fernsehen watching TV
Filzstift felt tip
Fisch fish
Freund, Freundin friend
Freunde treffen meeting friends
Frohe Weihnachten! Merry
  Christmas!
Füller pen
fünf five

G (fünfzig...)

fünfzig fifty
Fußball football
Fußball spielen playing football

G

Gartenhaus garden shed
Geburtstag birthday
Geburtstagsgeschenk birthday
  present
Geburtstagskarte birthday card
Geburtstagskuchen birthday cake
gehen go
gelb yellow
Getränk drink
glücklich happy
grau grey
groß big
Großvater grandfather
Großmutter grandmother
grün green
gut good

H

Hallo! Hello!
Hamster hamster
Handschuhe gloves
Haus house
Haustier pet
Heiligabend (24.12.) Christmas Eve
Hemd shirt
**Herzlichen Glückwunsch zum
  Geburtstag!** Happy Birthday!
hinter behind
Hobby hobby
Hose trousers
Hund dog
hundert hundred
hungrig hungry

I

in in
Inlineskates inline skates

J

Jacke jacket
Jeans jeans
Junge boy

K

kalt cold
Kaninchen rabbit
Katze cat
Kerze candle
Kirsche cherry
Klasse class

Klassenzimmer classroom
Klebestift glue stick
Kleid dress
klein small
kommen come
können can

L
Laden shop
langweilig boring
Lehrer, Lehrerin teacher
lesen read
Lieblings- favourite
Lineal ruler

M
Mädchen girl
Maus mouse
Meerschweinchen guinea pig
Milch milk
Mittagessen lunch
mögen like
Möhre carrot
Musik hören listening to music
Mutter mother
Mütze hat

N
Name name
neben next to
neun nine
neunzig ninety

O
Obst fruit
Orange, orange orange
Osterei Easter egg
Osterhase Easter bunny
Osterkorb Easter basket
Ostern Easter

P
Pfirsich peach
Pflaume plum
Pfund (£) pound
Pullover pullover

R
Radiergummi rubber
Ratte rat
Rock skirt
Roller scooter
rosa pink
rot red

S
Saft juice
Salat lettuce
Schere scissors
Schlafzimmer bedroom
Schokolade chocolate
Schuhe shoes
Schule school
Schultasche school bag
schwarz black
Schwester sister
sechs six
sechzig sixty
sehr very
sieben seven
siebzig seventy
Skateboard skateboard
Socken socks
spielen play
Stuhl chair

T
T-Shirt T-shirt
toll great
Tomate tomato
trinken drink
Tschüss! Bye!

U
unter under

V
Vater father
vier four
vierzig forty
vor in front of

W
Weihnachten Christmas
Weihnachtsbaum Christmas tree
Weihnachtsmann Father Christmas
Weihnachtstag (25.12.) Christmas
  Day
weiß white
Wohnzimmer living room

Z
Zahl number
zehn ten
zeichnen draw
Zimmer room
Zitrone lemon
zwanzig twenty
zwei two